Designed and edited by Stu Waldman and Marty Goldstein
Copyright © 1987 by Jill Freedman
All rights reserved under International and Pan-American
Copyright Conventions.
Published by Friendly Press, Inc., 401 Park Avenue South,
New York, New York 10016
Printed and bound in Spain by Heraclio Fournier, S.A.
End paper photo by Earl Culberson

Library of Congress Cataloging in Publication Data
Freedman, Jill.
    A time that was.
    1. Ireland—Description and travel—1981–
Views.   I. Title.
DA982.F74   1987   941.50824   87-361
ISBN 0-914919-09-1

A Time That Was

A Time That Was

Irish Moments by Jill Freedman

I dedicate this book with love and appreciation to
my father and mother
Ross and Selma Shaeffer Freedman, Aaron Siskind, Pat Phildy McGowan, Jack Deacy,
Vincent, Angela and Kieran Moloney, Sean McCarthy, and Dr. Johnny Walsh.
The like of them will never be again.

Introduction

My love affair with Ireland began years before I ever picked up a camera.
When I was in college I discovered Yeats, Joyce, Synge, O'Casey, O'Connor, O'Faolain.
Their words and melodies struck a chord deep within me. It was visceral.
They reminded me strongly of the great Yiddish writers.
They too sang of the old days which were gone forever;
a way of life that would never return.

Later, after I had finished school and was living and singing in London,
I went over to Ireland for a week-end of traditional music.
Nothing could have prepared me for the strong emotions I felt there,
and I feel it each time I return.
As soon as I set foot on the land, I feel that I am home.
People often ask me if I'm Irish. After we establish
to their delight and satisfaction that I haven't a drop of Irish blood in my veins
("What about your great grandfather? Your great, great grandfather?"),
many tell me that I lived there in another life. I tell them I know.
"Are you home for long?" they ask. "Not long enough," I say.

That first visit was in 1962, in Mullingar, and I remember that the great piper,
Seamus Ennis, fell through the floor of the barn,
there were so many people crowded around listening to the music.
I also noticed that I had seen no fights, though drink was taken.
And it was a few days later, on a sunny June day in Dublin, that someone
played Sean O'Riada's recording of Playboy of the Western World for me,
and my case was closed.
I was forever in thrall to the music.
I went back the next year, too, for more of it, and it filled me like a good meal,
but stuck to the ribs, and kept me going much longer.

I didn't get back for another ten years, after I had at last found photography.
Pictures were my music now, and the camera was so much smaller than a guitar.
Again I went to hear the music,
and again I fell head over heels in love with the place and the people.
For a people *are* the place, even though the beauty of the land is astounding.

There was no age gap. Young and old alike enjoyed themselves in simple ways,
making music, gossiping, dancing sets. I would watch the old men in pubs
chatting away like there was no tomorrow, after seventy years of yesterdays,
and wonder what they could be talking about.
They had gone through life together in this little town,
and still there was always something to say. They never stopped talking.
It was there I learned the pleasure of good conversation.

I loved the gentleness, the sweet shyness, the warm welcomes and farewells,
the soda bread warm from the hearth, and always a sup to eat and drink.
The pleasure they had in welcoming a stranger, who left a friend.

The old ways were still in evidence.
Donkey carts taking milk to the dairy, gathering the hay, market days in small towns.
(These are mostly gone now, replaced by co-ops and auctions.)
The women on one side of the pub, the men on the other, generations dancing together.
People making their own music,
playing pipes, fiddles, flutes, melodeons, penny whistles, guitars, mouths, bones.

I spent a week listening to the great fiddler Johnny Dougherty in Donegal
and have his image forever preserved on paper and in my heart.
He died three years later,
and each time I look at his picture,I realize again the magic of photography.
There he is, caught the instant after delivering a funny line
and starting right in on his tune.
I figure if you get ten pictures like this in your whole life, you're lucky.

Seven years were to go by until I could get back, and the changes were disturbing.
I have no romantic illusions about poverty.
Everybody wants a built-in toilet, a warm room, nice clothes, enough food.
But the qualitative differences! The difference between coal and turf.
The warmth, the smell of the turf fire enclosing you,
the earthy smoke of the peat, as opposed to coal fumes.
But the old people can't dig the turf anymore and the young ones don't bother.
So now Babby has a gas stove and buys her bread from the grocer,
because you need a turf fire to bake a decent soda bread.
Always there was the welcoming loaf. Now there is white plastic bread.

I remembered the ham and cabbage.
The old ones went out to their gardens and pulled up some potatoes,
added a cabbage, and put in that good Irish ham.
And you had a meal you never forgot, nothing ever tasted that good.
Now there is plastic ham, turkey roll and instant potatoes, just like here.
Margarine instead of butter.
And where once there was a nice cup of tea, now there are teabags in metal pots.
That is no way to drink tea.

I had caught the tail end of the old ways. Young and old
sitting together while the old ones passed on their oral history.
Tales of heroes and fairies passed around the fire the way it always had been.
Before the books and the television.
Before Dallas and the Love Boat.
Before television shrunk the world.
Now there are very few of the old shannachies (story tellers) left,
and most people don't seem to care.

Instead they have transistors blasting in the streets,
jukeboxes, radios, and tapes in pubs.
Musicians driven out of pubs by heavy metal noise and loud braying voices.
Loud clumsy sounds to accompany new clumsy dances.

There are many new houses, built alongside the old abandoned ones which, even
falling into ruin, have more grace than the boxes which replaced them.
Just like here, where each day one is confronted by some blank wall of windows
where once had stood a building of charm and individuality.

Beer cans in the lakes of Killarney.
Killarney a tourist mall; shilling leprechauns made in Japan.

Yet there are still places where old Ireland lives.
I found the Slieve Luachra mountains of Kerry and West Cork.
There in Dan O'Connell's pub people danced sets to music played as it was long ago,
when they danced the nights away in the kitchen.
I danced a series of wild Kerry sets with Dan O'Keefe, an eighty-two year old farmer,
that left me gasping for air and he spry as a young goat.
They told me that in Slieve Luachra, the men live to be a hundred,
and the women never die at all.

I became even more driven to record this traditional life. Like those who collect stories
from the shannachies, I am collecting moments. A jet plane is a far cry
from an immigrant ship. You can come home in hours now, not generations.
Who will remember the old ways?

I think of my work in Ireland as a love poem:
a celebration of the beauty of the land, the warmth of her people,
the simplicity of the old ways and traditions, the humor and conviviality,
the sharp wit and black moods, the kindness.
Today, our vision of that country is colored by the violence of the North or
the standard visual cliches: freckled kids in Irish sweaters; all those green, green fields.
It is an older, gentler Ireland I am documenting.
A wild and passionate beauty that I feel is the last place on earth. .

I want to get it down now, while there are still people
who remember a time that was, places that were, that will never be again.

Jill Freedman, New York City, 1987.

The Land

"There is some alchemy of climate in Ireland
that bedews the countryside with an unmistakable personality:
it is in the softness of color, the mobility of the light,
the gentleness with which sound caresses the ear."

Sean O'Faolain
An Irish Journey

Dingle,
County Kerry

Glenbeigh,
County Kerry

Connemara,
County Galway

Connemara,
County Galway

County Limerick

Connemara,
County Galway

Inisheer,
Aran Islands

The Life

"How I love the old town
where every man is a potential idler, poet or friend.
I love the old town
where sock-suspenders are less important than poems!
And directions depend on inns."

Oliver St. John Gogarty
As I Was Going Down Sackville Street

Gurteen,
County Sligo

Arigna,
County Roscommon

County Tipperary

Tawnylea,
County Leitrim

Ballyvourney,
County Cork

The first day of the hunting season.
　　Maire had been counting the days until she and the dog
　　would be out on the mountain hunting grouse.
　　It was a young dog and Maire was still teaching it,
　　but you could see the little bitch had heart.
　　She was fast and loved the praise.

We climbed into a mist, the ground soft and spongy,
past banks of heather and hills of yellow blossoms,
Moving over the mountain,
while below us the valley spread herself wide,
all wet with dew.

Doonagore,
County Clare

Gnivguilla,
County Kerry

Milltown Malbay,
County Clare

Tarbert,
County Kerry

Two old men talking. You see it everywhere,
the well-turned phrase, the funny story.
Soft-spoken, courteous, each enjoying the other.
Two old men, stopping to chat.

Fair Day

Drumkeeran,
County Leitrim

Men and sheep and cattle stood in clumps along
the one street. The men, in suits, white shirts and ties,
circulated, inspecting and discussing each animal.
There was wise counsel all around.
One man fancied a little black cow, and the ritual began.
The seller started high, the buyer started low.

One praising the strength of shoulder, the other remarking the shortness of leg.
"She gives the milk of two." "With ribs on her like the roof of a shed."
A third man joined in, urging them on, while an interested audience served as chorus.
Finally, the price agreed, the buyer spat on his palm, slapped the seller's hand,
and struck the bargain.

Fair Day

Drumkeeran,
County Leitrim

Fair Day

Dowra,
County Cavan

Fair Day

Drumkeeran,
County Leitrim

Fair Day

Drumkeeran,
County Leitrim

Look at this dog, his head barely raised.
        Not one sheep dares to stir. This dog has control and they know it.
        They act like a bunch of sheep.
        On fair day, a farmer can do his buying and selling,
        then enjoy himself in the pub until closing time,
        knowing that his dog is taking care of business.

Crevelea,
County Leitrim

Paddy the Poet and Spot live on the road to heaven,
    the long road that climbs up to the bog and on to the sky.
    It's quiet there, just the animals and the wind.
    When Paddy was young,
    the townlands were full of young people and music.
    They would ramble from house to house, singing, dancing, courting, joking.

One by one the young people left, and it was Paddy alone on the farm.
He never married. "I wasn't in the fettle for it."
The land is poor, the life hard, the world older, but he and his bachelor friends
are happy in their fellowship and possessions, wanting nothing more.
He's a happy man, kind to people as well as animals.

Crevelea,
County Leitrim

Paddy always loved to play
       tricks on people. Each summer
       when his nephew Jack visited from Brooklyn,
       he brought funny presents for Paddy,
       whoopee cushions, the fly in the plastic ice cube, plastic dog shit:
       Dumb stuff, but Paddy was delighted.

He'd invite a guest to sit by the fire and have some tea.
The guest would sit, the cushion would fart,
and Paddy would laugh and laugh.
Jack also would send him false faces.
Gorilla heads. Frankenstein. Dracula.
Paddy would go around to the neighbors after dark,
pretending to be a traveler, asking if he could stay the night.
When they'd open the door, they'd see a giant gorilla.
For Paddy it was great fun,
even though he met several dogs who did not share his sense of humor.
He wore his favorite face for me when I visited.
However, he didn't fool the cow.

Connemara,
County Galway

Dublin

Ballybunion,
County Kerry

His mother and his bride each have a grip on him.
     The men may play the fiddles, but the women call the tunes.
     My friend Kieran brought me along.
     The families welcomed me and insisted I sit down and eat.
     Two priests gave sermons.
     The brothers and the uncles read telegrams and made jokes.

The groom thanked everyone who was there, one by one, by one.
He thanked the hotel for the good feed.
There was a band, people danced, kids chased each other around.
Girls giggled, boys blushed, young women flirted, young men blushed,
and two people who had known each other all their lives had tied the iron knot.

Ballybunion,
County Kerry

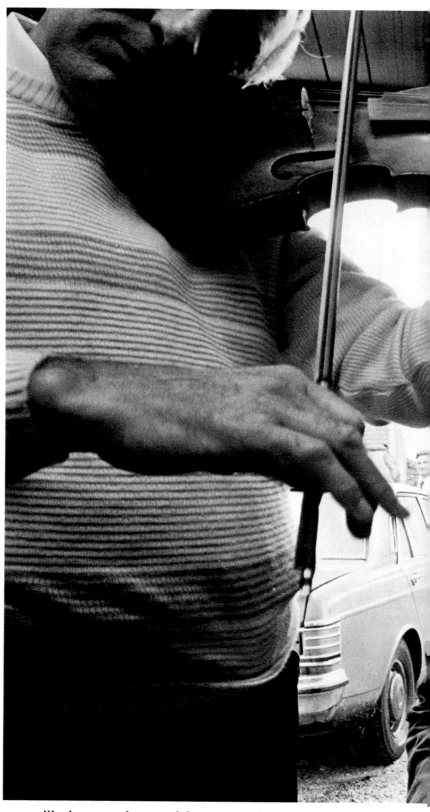

After the wedding, a dash across the road.
  A couple of pints and a few fast tunes will shorten the road between church and reception.
  Doctor Johnny told me about another wedding last September.
  He delivered the baby in March.

He said he smacked it on its bottom and cradled it in his arms.
The baby opened its eyes, saw the snow outside the window, and said,
"Jaysus, doc, 'tis chilly for June."

Crevelea,
County Leitrim

Drumkeeran,
County Leitrim

Gnivguilla,
County Kerry

Listowel,
County Kerry

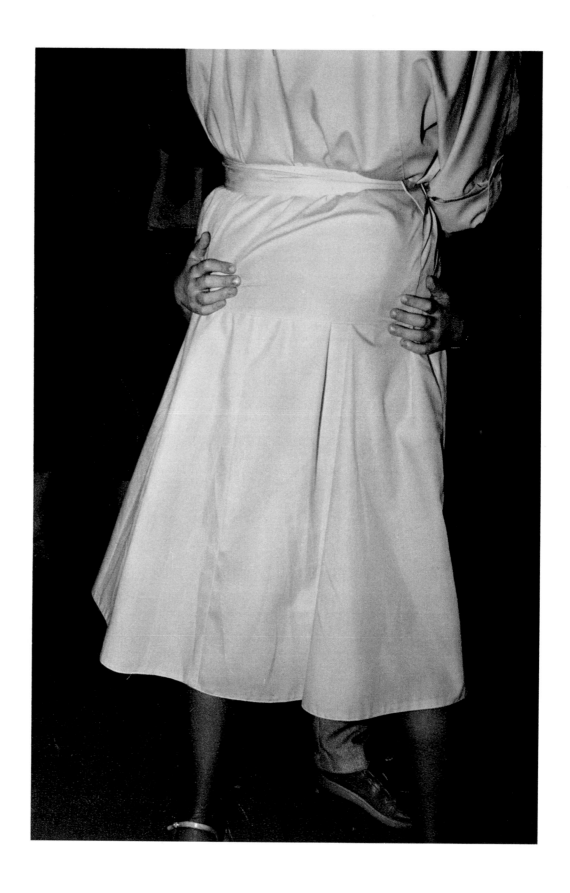

Dingle,
County Kerry

Dublin

Connemara,
County Galway

Listowel,
County Kerry

Davey and Maisie Gunn live in Listowel,
        a few miles outside of the town. You go down a road
        and up a boreen along some fields,
        and there's the cottage.

Maisie still drives her one milk churn into the dairy every day in her donkey cart.
If you're sitting in Moloney's pub,
you can see her through the lounge window, riding past.

Listowel,
County Kerry

Davey makes bodhrans; tambourines of goatskin
stretched over round wooden frames. Davey gets orders
for his bodhrans from all over the world,
and deadly serious percussionists often seek him out and sign his guest book.

Davey and Maisie have cared for each other for over forty years.
It's lovely to think of the two of them sitting there at night,
playing their music together.

Killarney,
County Kerry

Imagine swimming in the lakes of Killarney.
    Then staying the night on a dark lake island,
    hearing ghosts in the old manor ruin.
    Ghostly music where the ballroom once stood.
    Some say the ghosts were badgers.
    Others say nothing at all, and never go camping again.

Dowra,
County Cavan

Katie lives with Mylie, her oldest. She's a widow
and it's just the two of them below the two fields,
and the cats, dogs, sheep and chickens.
Mylie is great at training sheep dogs.
He'll never marry and leave his old mother.
"He's a good boy," Katie said.

Connemara,
County Galway

Finoog,
County Kerry

Country kids dreaming of becoming famous jockeys
start like this, in the little town races. Galloping around fields and along strands.
Going on to Punchestown, Leopardstown, Fairystown, Baldoyle.
Bigger and bigger stakes. Fame and fortune.

Listowel Races. The Galway Races. Phoenix Park.
Galloping into glory at the Curragh,
winning the Derby itself.

County Tipperary

Josie Conor. I first saw her walking up a hill
        with a sack of coal over her shoulder. We drove her home,
        and the son of the house said she was one hundred and two.
        Which meant somewhere in her nineties.
        A little girl's freckled face, in her nineties.

County Tipperary

She and her sister had married, raised families,
were widowed, and here they were, back living as girls together
in the cottage. Just like they had started out.
An old Model-T was their chickencoop;
they supped out of rose-covered teacups.

They had a little black cat, the sister wore a white apron,
and later in the pub, Josie tossed back a pint with pleasure and ease.
"I'm the best woman in the five counties,
and I've scrubbed more floors, inside and out."

County Tipperary

The Music

"A tune is more lasting than the song of the birds,
a word is more lasting than the riches of the world."

Irish Proverb

Doolin,
County Clare

Micho Russell is a farmer well-known for his
 whistle-playing. Sometimes he hears a tune in the wind.
  "Like some kind of fairy music," he said.
  "It might be coming in on a concertina or a whistle,
   or whatever'd be playing around the caves and cliffs.
   And I'd pick it up that way."

He sits on the Pipers Chair,
an ancient rock in his field overlooking the cliffs of Moher.
There is a fairy ring around it.
Some say they've heard the pipes, and seen the fairies glowing in the moonlight,
dancing round and round the rock.

Carrick,
County Donegal

The great Johnny Dougherty,
who spent his life travelling the roads and rarely left Donegal.
The Doughertys knew every inch and by-road of the county
and were welcome everywhere, a place at the table and before the fire,
and honor on the house they visited.
For to hear them fiddle was to forget all your cares and sorrows.

I spent a week with him in Carrick, Donegal, in the company of two friends,
accordion players, each so delighted whenever they met between gigs
that time was vanquished and they drank and played together
until one or the other had to go.
Thus was born one of the happiest weeks of my life.
For Johnny was above praise, above words, he was a miracle,
and lucky the one who could sit and listen.
Johnny was staying in a little room above the Doc's pub,
where the women fed and looked after him.
He was seventy at the time, and he played every day to the pleasure of the locals
who attended him in rapt silence.
"Sure, 'tis only the ignorant who talk while great music is played."
There was no talking in the Doc's pub.
The music would begin in the afternoon and go until two in the morning.
They took turns, first the old man, then the boys,
the notes and spirits rising higher and higher tune by tune.
When Johnny Dougherty fiddled, sure there was nowhere else you wanted to be.
First he would tell a little story, or maybe just give an introduction,
and then he'd play.
His voice was as sweet as his fiddle.
This went on the whole week, with the soft mist outside
and the warm whiskey inside, and if I had died then, I would have died happy.
Johnny died four years later, but I hear him still,
the punchline and the laughter, the sweet smile,
the great musician's sure timing, striking to the heart of humor,
to the heart of music, to the wild delicious joy of life.

Spiddal,
County Galway

Lisdoonvarna,
County Clare

Knocknagree,
County Cork

Bridgie Kelleher, age ninety.
        She bore thirteen children and raised eleven,
        all of whom emigrated except for the one son in Tralee.
        She's the sister of two legendary Kerry fiddlers, the late Dennis Murphy,
        and Julia Clifford, who lives in England.

She told me stories of her youth, of Dennis and Julia fiddling down at the crossroads,
and she herself dancing the wild Kerry sets.
Bridgie was a great dancer in her day, she never sat one out,
and there were few who could keep up with her.
She told me about the house parties, too.
The tables and chairs would be pushed against the wall
and they'd dance the nights away in the kitchen.
They made their own good times in those days, and part of the fun
was running out the back door when the priest came on a raid.
The road to hell was traveled by dancing feet,
and that made it even more fun.
Julia was home for the summer and we had a great session one night down in West Cork.
The man of the house was a flute player and Julia told many tales on her fiddle.
On the way home Bridgie said, "The music was great but the people didn't dance.
I hate to see the music go to waste."

Knocknagree,
County Cork

County Clare

Listowel,
County Kerry

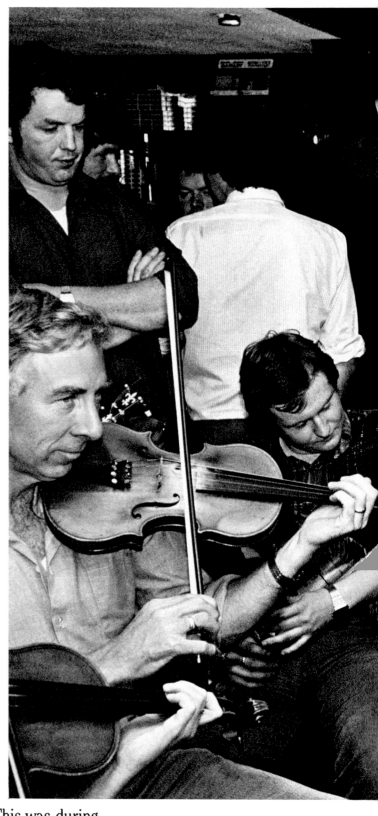

A great session in Vincent and Angela Moloney's pub,
where no musician goes hungry or thirsty. This was during
a fleadh cheoil, or traditional music festival.
Thousands of musicians, amateur and professional, come
to test themselves in the competitions and to give or take classes,

and for three days every street and lane and pub rings with singing and
dancing and the playing of instruments. It is three days of drinking and music,
telling tales and spinning yarns, grabbing a bite and falling into bed,
and starting again, then crawling out and starting again.

Listowel,
County Kerry

Here is my great friend Angela Moloney.
The man she is hugging is from Baltimore, West Cork.
He has the gift of healing in his big hands;
he is the bone setter.
His dead mother, dressed all in white,
came to him one night in a dream and told him he had the gift.

Mullach,
County Clare

Arigna,
County Roscommon

Packy Dignan, an Arigna miner, and Patsy Hanley
are playing under a tea-towel that bears the ancient Irish blessing,
"May you be in heaven one hour before the Devil knows you are dead."

Lisdoonvarna,
County Clare

The Pub

"He who would give up drink is a foolish person."

Carolan the Blind Harper
18th Century

Dowra,
County Cavan

A good pub. The slow
black stout and the nut brown ale.
Drinking deeply, here where it was first distilled, the waters of life,
that humane and lyrical gift to the world.
A pub without jukebox or stereo or tv,
where the music of human discourse need not be shouted over an incessant din.

A quiet pub, where you can drink the holy waters
and vanquish the Sin of Loneliness.
A sanctuary where you can contemplate the eternal mysteries,
the publican a shield between you and the outside world.
It is the center of social life,
a place to relax, cash checks, borrow money,
give and get messages, meet friends, gossip.
Moods are respected here.
You may start off solitary, and as the second pint
flows gently into your bloodstream,
you can dive into a swelling flood of friends,
bosom buddies you may never see again.
Nothing is asked but good manners.
The night wears on, and before you know it,
the wit is flowing freely as the drink, rapier thrusts of wit,
machine gun blasts of rhethoric, cute and sly stilettos.
The gentle art of conversation played as a game of wits,
and you can sharpen your own while you're at it.
Or just listen.
A Killarney man once told me, "If you can't dazzle them with brilliance,
baffle them with bullshit."

Finoog,
County Kerry

Finoog,
County Kerry

A man and his old dog having a quiet pint together,
sitting under a fish that was too good to eat.

Milltown Malbay,
County Clare

Milltown Malbay,
County Clare

Dublin

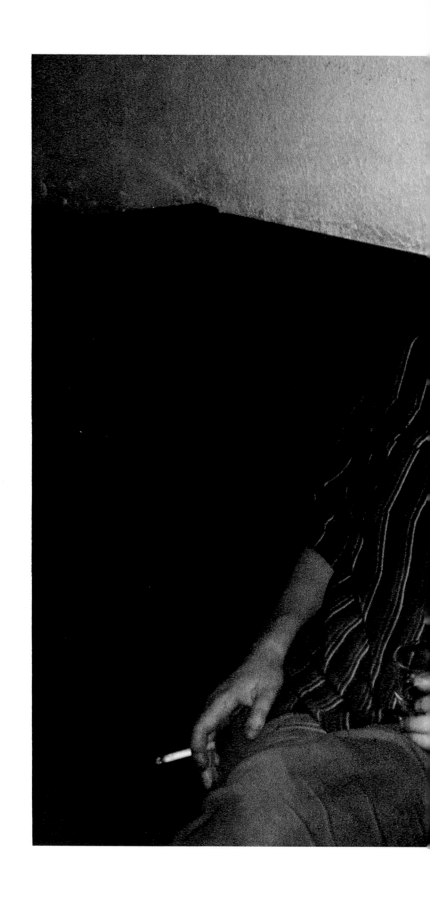

Finoog,
County Kerry

Every now and then,
    Tom Sheehan brings his pony into the pub for a pint.
    The pony is an old pet and he loves his pint.
    See how sensuously he closes his eyes,
    how delicately he drinks,
    the hairs on his chin quivering with pleasure.